# Make A Joyful Noise

## By Mendi Joi Wilson

Designed/Arranged by Demetrius H. Carter

Poems to encourage the heart, mind, and soul.

"Make a joyful shout to the Lord,

all you lands!" Psalm 100:1

## Mendi Joi Wilson

## Edited by Lorna Joy Larkin

ISBN: 978-0-9834193-1-0

# DEDICATION

To God who has inspired me to write.

To my mother who has been and always will be my #1 fan.

To my family, my church family, and friends who have

supported me along this journey.  I thank you!

# CONTENTS

# ACKNOWLEDGMENTS

Psalm 100: "Make a joyful shout to the LORD, all you lands! Serve the LORD with gladness; Come before His presence with singing. Know that the LORD, He is God; it is He who has made us, and not we ourselves; we are His people and the sheep of His pasture. Enter into His gates with thanksgiving, and into His courts with praise. Be thankful to Him, and bless His name. For the LORD is good; His mercy is everlasting, and His truth endures for all generations."

"Make A Joyful Noise" is a collection of poems geared to warm the heart and mind of the reader. The poems are inspired by God and are an outpour of the author's heart. The poems are meant to encourage, inspire, and value the love of God and relationships. It demonstrates pains experienced, as well as hope, that better days are to come. Five themes are represented:

Salvation is the FREE gift from God to anyone who comes to Him and desires to live for Him.

Honor those who are important to you because they can be gone in an instant. Appreciate those you love now so that there will be no regrets when they are gone. Do right by others so that you can leave behind a legacy for those after you to cherish and model.

We all have feelings just waiting to be released. Feelings of loneliness, hurt, despair, are valid feelings. The longer we hold onto these negative feelings, the more damaging it is to our ability to cope and our relationships with others. They can take root and damage us emotionally if not released.

God created us for relationships. Although some people are in our lives for a season, others for a reason, and still others for a lifetime, we are not meant to be in this world or go through life alone. We are to value the relationships we have for the time we have them.

Dare to dream, dare to love. For some, love comes easy and for others, it's a struggle. But love is the greatest gift God gave to us and He wants us to experience it too! Guard your heart, but don't close yourself off completely to others. Take your time, choose wisely, and be careful! Love is a beautiful thing if not abused!

God loves us so much that He created us with a purpose in mind. We owe it to ourselves and to Him to live out that purpose. Not only will we be blessed, but we'll also be a blessing to others and God will get the glory. We're all special, we're all unique. Live, laugh, love! Have fun being the beautiful you that you are!

# You Don't Know

You don't know when your time will come

So get up, get out and have some fun.

But be careful of what you say and do,

'Cause God the Father has His eyes on you.

You might fool others and even yourself,

Not God for He knows you like no one else.

Be slow to anger and slow to speak;

Ask God to help you when you are weak.

Don't repay evil with evil;

But be patient, wait, and be still.

Get yourself right before God and with others;

Love your enemies, your sisters and your brothers.

For God is love this we know is true;

When you do wrong, He finds peace with you,

As long as you repent for your sins

And hold on tight through thick and thin.

No one said it would be easy, all you gotta do is try;

God will make Himself known—His Word, it does not lie.

Know who you are, where you're going, and where you're coming

From, for no one knows when his hour will come!

3

# Look To Jesus

Many people die to self

While others die to sin;

They get caught up in the pleasures of the world

And have no peace within.

Money is nice

But it doesn't always last;

You need someone to forgive your wrongs

And to forget about your past.

Trust in God

For He's always there;

When your friends forsake you,

It is God who cares.

People will come

And people will go;

When you die,

Only God knows.

Tomorrow is not promised

And hell is real;

Knowing where you'll be

Is a very big deal.


God loves you

And He wants you to come

Can't no one else save you,

You must save yourself from


All the evils in the world

That stretch far and wide;

Look to Jesus

For He is your guide!

# You Don't Know (Part 2)

You don't know what tomorrow will bring;

You don't know whether to laugh or sing.

Pick up your burdens and place them at the altar;

He is Thy Lord, Your God, the Everlasting Father.


Do it now for tomorrow is too late;

Get right before God, don't even hesitate.

For He loves you and wants you to be with Him

Hurry up or you'll die in sin.


Choosing to ignore will only put you to demise;

Satan will sneak right in and take you by surprise.

Hell is real and the devil is too;

When you're not careful, he will attack you.


So know God's Word and apply it to your life.

He'll heal your pain and take away your strife.

Surrender today so you can be free;

'Cause in Him there's victory!

# Who Are You?

Who are you to smile in my face only to talk behind my back as we pass?

Who are you to steal from the poor and rape little children?

Who are you to praise God in church on Sundays then do this, that, and the other the rest of the week?

Who are you to worship idols, such as material things, rather than the One who created **all** things?

Who are you to gossip about other people's problems when you can't take care of your own?

Who are you to always point fingers at others instead of looking in the mirror to examine yourself?

Who are you to poke fun at those less fortunate instead of lending a helping hand or a listening ear?

Who are you to be quick to anger instead of taking time to relax, think, and then respond?

Who are you to judge a problem instead of trying to find a solution?

Who are you to lie in a court of law instead of admitting your faults?

Who are you to cheat on your spouse instead of living out the vows you both made before God?

Who are you to kill innocent people for things you don't have instead of working hard to earn them?

Who are you to lust over another person's mate instead of waiting on God to send you His best?

Who are you to disrespect anyone whom you feel instead of respecting everyone?

Who are you to hate because of ignorance instead of trying to get to know everyone's differences?

Who are you to pretend to love someone when you really don't?

Who, you ask?

Well, my friend, that WHO is sin!

# Trust Me

When you are down, My child,

Look up for I am here.

When your friends are gone,

Call Me, for I am near.

Bring your problems,

Great and small;

One-by-one

I will handle them all.

Yes, no, or wait

I will say;

Open your heart

So you can receive Me.

I've loved you since before your birth.

I love you now and forevermore

For all you are worth.

I don't care what

You've gone through or where you've been.

I will erase your past

And relieve you from sin.

Bring all your burdens,

Give them to me now

Trust Me, My child

This is my solemn vow.

# The Good News

It took One who had no sin

To die for sin

So that we would no longer

Live in sin and be dead to sin

In order to be free from sin.


Do you know of any other

Who would risk his life for his brother?

A sinless Man who paid the price

And gave up His life as the ultimate sacrifice?


This He did on that first day;

He hung His head and bled on Good Friday.

To stay dead was merely a farce,

For in three days He rose again on Sunday

And to this day,

He reigns forevermore!

# Count It All Joy

Count it all joy

When you're going through,

Don't let your circumstances

Get the best of you.

Trials and tribulations

Will come your way,

You must believe and not doubt

When you ask and pray.


Sometimes you will suffer;

Sometimes you will cry,

But in the end

It's your flesh that must die.

Just keep on believing

For Jesus is near;

Don't ever give up,

You gotta persevere.

Trials will come

But it's for the best;

You'll be stronger in the end

When you pass the test.

Be thankful for each day,

Be it good or bad.

Rejoice in the Lord

And be continually glad!

# Armor of God

Be strong in the Lord

And use all your might

Satan is busy and

There's a battle you must fight.


Fight not with your hands

Nor with your feet

The enemy is near

It is he you must beat.


You won't be alone

When the devil attacks

Love the Lord, your God

For He has your back.


But always be ready

For Satan's busy schemes

Putting on the full armor of God

Will protect you from all enemies.

There is the belt of truth

Wrapped around your waist

And the breastplate of righteousness

Full of mercy and grace.


You have the gospel of peace

That is fitted firmly on your feet

And the shield of faith

To guard you against defeat.


Don't forget the helmet of salvation

To protect you at all costs

And the sword of the Spirit

To separate you from the lost.


Now to top it off with prayer

Make your requests known to God

For He knows **all** things

No more hiding behind your façade.

Now gird up your mind

And put the devil under your feet

With these seven weapons

Your armor is now complete!

# His Loving Grace

Jesus is in you and me,

We may not see Him

But He's there you see.


He is the Way, the Truth, and the Life;

With this in mind,

You need not fight.


For He died on the Cross to save our souls;

Why, you ask?

Only God knows.


He is wonderful, marvelous, magnificent,

The Creator, the Deliverer, and the Healer;

Our God Almighty is indeed omniscient.


There's nothing too hard for God to do;

He delivered Daniel

And He'll do the same for me and for you.

Jesus is alive

And according to Him,

You too shall survive.


When no one else seems to care,

Or nothing else seems to matter,

Look to God because He's always there.


As long as God is on His throne,

And you keep Him by your side,

You shall never, ever be alone.


Watch what you say

And be careful of what you do,

'Cause God the Father has His eyes on you.


Don't take what you've heard

From those darn non-believers;

Instead, open the Bible for in every word

There is a lesson to be learned.  Worrying is a sin,

But you don't have to fret

When you keep God within.


Get yourself together

Before you can walk with King Jesus,

So that you can have a life of peace and harmony in Heaven forever.


Don't be afraid to ask Him for advice;

His arms, hands, legs, and feet were nailed to the Cross,

For that can't you sacrifice?


Don't ever be ashamed to leave Earth;

If it is God's will for you to be with Him,

This He knew since your birth.


Only God knows the time and place

When you'll leave your family and friends.

So live life to the fullest and await His loving grace!

# THE CALL

With sin all around us

It can't be stopped

Stealing our joy,

Adding pain to our hearts,

Ripping our families apart

Praise GOD for the LOVE that CHRIST gave

He substituted His love for the evil that Satan intended

To kill, steal, and destroy

That is his goal

And even when the pain doesn't seem to end

God is right there to hold you in His arms, my friend


We all have the power to change the world

To reach every man, woman, boy, and girl

With the gospel of Jesus

We can save the lost

So give your life to Christ,

For there is no cost

Salvation is the greatest free gift

One could ever receive

All you have to do is love Jesus with all your heart

And believe

That He died on the Cross for you and me

So that we can live peacefully in eternity


Satan and his boys will be put to demise

When Jesus returns

So give Him your life today

Or you too will burn

Do it today, please do it now

For tomorrow is not guaranteed

Who cares what your friends may say

Let go of your pride

He will fulfill all the voids

That lies deep down inside

We all want to go to Heaven

But there's only one way

So give Him your life

Please do it today

I say this to you because I care

I won't judge you, point the finger or the blame

For I say all these things in Jesus' Name

When you answer the call

Your life will never be the same

As a new creature

He'll give you a new name

Ladies and gentlemen, my family, my friends

He's knocking on the door of your heart

Will you let Him in?

Be brave, stand proud, and stand tall

He's waiting on you to answer the call!

# 'Til We Meet Again

You have gone

To a whole new place,

Leaving your family and friends behind.

It was beyond your control

Because God said, "It's time!"

And even that you can't argue.


The thought of you leaving

Makes me very sad and afraid.

But knowing that you're now at peace

Makes my heart a little more at ease.

No more fear, no more pain, no more suffering

In this crude, sick world in which I live.


I often ask the question, "why you, Lord?"

But all He says is that it was your time.

Yet, so young, so innocent, so beautiful

And so many mistakes left to be made.

You were just a child,

And just like that you were taken away.

I wish we could've grown closer,

Instead God deprived me of that opportunity.

No more hugs and no more laughs.

Worst of all, I didn't get to say goodbye.

But what you left me with are good memories,

I couldn't ask God for anything more.


This poem is a little message from me to you

From the bottom of my heart,

To let you know that you are certainly missed

And when God is ready for me to leave,

I'll await the arrival of seeing you only in Heaven,

'Til we meet again!

# Tribute To Daymon

Once you were here bringing joy to the earth.

Once you were here earning all your money's worth.


You were always respectful, patient, and kind.

You worked hard and kept others in mind.


But one awful Saturday night,

You were hit without a fight.


One shot was all it took,

Now your name is written in the Book.


Never again will we see your smiling face.

Never again will we feel your warm embrace.


I wish it didn't have to end;

You were a loving son, brother, and friend.


Wish we had some answers, Lord tell us please.

All we have now are just fond memories.

We must put a stop to all the violence in the world

That's killing all our men, women, little boys, and girls.


This is a prayer from me to you

Rest in peace, Daymon and may God continually bless you!

# 26 Angels

One awful Friday morning,
A spray of bullets is all it took
To annihilate **26** angels
At Sandy Hook.

They went to school
Like any normal day,
Only to fall to their demise
In a horrible way.

They had nowhere to hide
And nowhere to run;
A mad man came in
And stole all the fun.

There were 20 children

Learning at best,

As 6 adults tried

To protect the rest.


Now Newport, Connecticut

Will never be the same;

With pictures of their beautiful faces

No one will forget their names.


Hearts are broken

And families are torn,

No chance to say good-bye

Left them forlorn.

What a horrible scene
And an awful sight;
Now there stands 26 angels
To protect them each night.

Let's not forget the valiant, heroic efforts of
Dawn, Mary, Lauren, Victoria,
Rachel, & Anne who selflessly sacrificed
themselves to protect as many as they could
from that evil man.

God brought home
20 children, ages six and seven,
And although they were only on
Earth a short time,
Their new home is now in Heaven.

As we remember

Each smile, hug, and bundle of joy,

Take time to spread love throughout the world

To every man, woman, girl, and boy!

MY PERSONAL FEELINGS CHART

# Alone

Alone is the feeling of emptiness,

A loss of hope and despair.

Alone is knowing that you are all by yourself

And no one else seems to care.


Alone is being in complete solitude,

With no one to talk to.

Alone is seeing your goals fail,

And never having anything to do.


Alone is not knowing who you can turn to

Or who you can trust;

Alone is not knowing who your "true" friends are,

If you have any at all for that matter.


Alone is when you give your all

And get nothing in return.

Alone is not finding any happiness within yourself,

And you cry all night long.

Alone is the feeling of worthlessness,

And that everything you do is wrong.

Alone is always putting yourself down

Because you have no one to pick you up.


Alone is a feeling that you'd rather be in a hole somewhere

Than to be here with the rest of the world.

Alone is you thinking about dying

More now than ever before.


Alone is not being afraid of death;

To you, even that is better than being well and alive.

Alone is always questioning

Why God wants you to survive.

# Take Me Away

No more drugs

And no more gangs;

I'm sick of seeing

The same 'ol thangs.


Everyone is sick,

And everyone is lost;

Lord, please help them see

Who's the real Boss!


I'm tired of being hungry;

I'm tired of being poor.

All the sins I'm forced to live

I would much rather ignore.


Lord, I don't understand

Why you hate me so.

I haven't done anything wrong

So why do I feel so low?

This madness is more

Than I can take.

Please spare my life

For Heaven's sake!


It never seems to go away

The pain I feel inside;

I really don't know what to do

These burdens I cannot hide.


I wish I could disappear

From all the sins of the world.

All I want is to live my life,

For I am just a little girl.


I don't want to hurt anymore,

And I no longer want to stay

In this crude, sick world,

Lord, please, just take me away!

# Crumbling

I can't breathe

I hurt all over

I utter words but I cannot speak;

I exist but I am not living.

The pain I feel is unbearable.

When will it end?

When will this storm subside?

How much more can I possibly take?


My heart is crumbling deep down inside

I want to run but I cannot hide;

I cannot face another day,

Trapped in darkness, I cannot find my way.

I pray for peace, love, and understanding,

But instead this pain is so demanding.

This load I'm carrying is too much to bear

So on bended knee I kneel in prayer.

Lord, please take this pain away

So I can be free and live for today,

For tomorrow is not promised I know to be true,

But this sting keeps me from loving you

To the fullest and to my deepest capacity,

I want to love you with all tenacity.


Lord, please take this pain away

In my own strength, I have nothing left to give

I need You to show me how to live.

Display in me Your peace that surpasses all understanding and

Guard my heart from all the sins that are so demanding.

You have the power to reassemble my broken pieces.

I will wait, for my crumbling heart will be no more.

With Your power, I will be restored

Back to life and be whole once more.

# Feelings

What do you feel when you look at me?

What do you think about when you kiss me?


I wish that you would talk to me and tell me how you feel,

Then my heart would be at ease and the truth revealed.


I no longer want to hide the feelings that lie deep down inside,

But the thought of us together makes me want to cry.


I feel that you have not been real with me,

What's holding you back from being close to me?


You tell me that you want to do this, that, and the other

But then you say one thing and do another.


I can't tell if you're serious or just a flirt;

Either way, I don't want to get hurt.


So please do us both a favor and search deep down within,

Do you really want to be my man or only just a friend?

Whatever it is you're feeling, I will try to understand;

But right now, the unknown is difficult for me to stand.

It's so important to know how you feel,

If what we have now is fake or real.

Be true to yourself and to me,

Just let me know how you're feeling.

# RELATIONSHIPS

# What Is This Thing?

What is this thing

That we call love?

One that was sent

From Heaven up above?

The first time we talked

I wanted to scream;

Could it be so, is this

Really the man of my dreams?

You prayed for me, sang to me,

And said all the right things.

Heck, you even talked about

Buying me a friendship ring!


You drove 12 long hours

Through the snow and sleet.

A month and a half had passed

And finally we would meet.

I couldn't wait to see your face

And wrap you in my arms.

I thought you'd say something funny,

And entice me with your charm.

Instead we argued all the time,

And we would often disagree;

You talked to your folks at home

More than you talked to me.

I asked, "what's the matter

Don't you like what you see?"

You wouldn't even hold my hand

Let alone, kiss me.


I once prayed to God

That He'd send me someone true,

And what I thought was real

He revealed the real you.

If only we had done it right

And started out as friends,

Perhaps we wouldn't be in this mess

Nor be close to the end.

Now we barely speak

Which I don't understand.

I wish that you would step up

And be a real God-fearing Christian man,

One who would admit his flaws

And apologize when wrong.

It's okay if you don't like me

Just please, don't drag me along.


I'm sorry that we didn't work

It really is a shame;

I'm not saying that it's all your fault

For I am equally to blame.

Now God has stepped in

To reveal the truth about us,

That this so-called love I thought

We shared, was really only lust.

Contrary to what you may think

From the contents of this letter,

I really do care for you

But right now, this is for the better.

I pray that you will be consumed

With extreme Holy Ghost fire;

May God bless you and keep you,

And give you your heart's desire!

# Free

Words cannot express how I truly feel

The guilt, the shame

My mind won't be still


The feelings I have for you

I can no longer hide

Stretching far and wide from the inside

Out, farther than the ocean blue

Oh how my heart just longs for you.


If only my heart and my mind would agree,

I could soar like an eagle and be free

Free to love, free to give, free to feel

What is meant to be my God will reveal

If only it were you

My heart would be at ease

Who am I to be with

Lord tell me please

I don't know how much more I can take

Loving this man or that man

I don't want to be fake

If I could choose it would be you

But most of all I want to be true

True to my heart, my God, and to thee

Please understand

And let me be free.

# Shame On Me

Shame on me to think that someone like you could ever truly love like someone like me.

Shame on me for believing in you when no one else did.

Shame on me to trust that you had my best interest at heart and to think I was important to you.

Shame on me for making myself available and coming to your rescue each time you called.

Shame on me for believing your every word.

Shame on me for lifting you up when everyone else was putting you down.

Shame on me for seeing the good in you.

Shame on me for thinking of you day in day out.

Shame on me for loving too hard.

Shame on me for giving you my heart

# SELF-WORTH

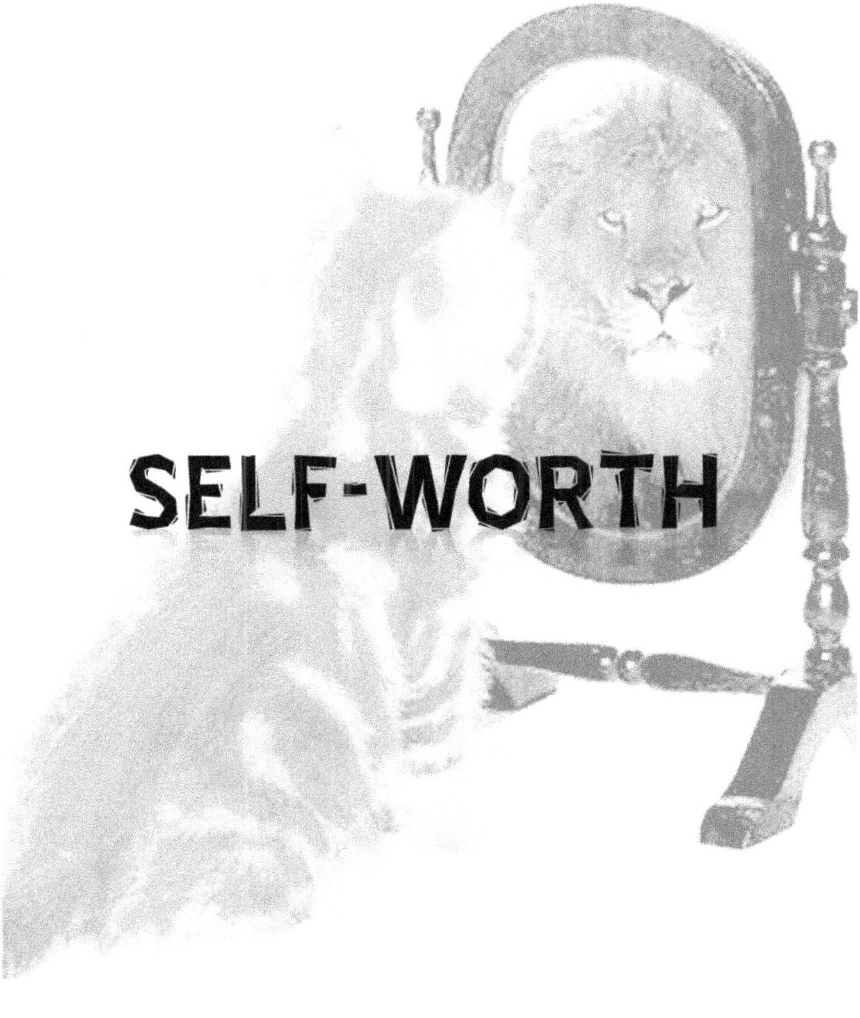

# I Am What I Am

**I am what I am**

Because God made me.

I may not be the prettiest;

I may not be the smartest,

But I am special to Him.

He loves me the way I am;

He sees what's inside.

The outside is not as important

As what's in the heart.

# In His Eyes

Even if I don't win accolades or applause from others,

I still am great and beloved to my Father.

In His eyes I am precious and worth far more than gold;

In His eyes I am loved more than ever told,

Like a rose that never withers or dies,

Or the sun that is always on the rise,

Is His love for me let the truth be told;

His eternal mercy will never grow old.

Oh how grateful am I for Thee,

Who loves me in spite of myself unconditionally;

No matter what I do or what I say,

My God is there to carry me along the way,

To guide my steps and catch me when I fall,

With open arms He welcomes me each time I call;

In His eyes I am loved let the truth be told;

In His eyes I am precious worth far more than gold;

He won't let me fail or be defeated,

Taken advantage of or be mistreated.

He encourages me to be the best that I can be

Because He loves me now and for all eternity!

# The Beautiful Me

When I look into the mirror,
I don't always like what I see.
But I know that's the devil
Speaking lies to me.

He tells me I'm not good enough
Or worthy to be loved
But real beauty is from within
And it's sent from God above.

I may not be the prettiest
But that's okay
You see to God I am special
And He loves me in every way.

He created me beautiful
No need to be fake
I'm fearfully & wonderfully made
God does not make mistakes.

When you look my way

You may not like what you see

But I love me anyway

I am the beautiful me!

# God Ain't Through With Me Yet!

I don't care what you think about me,

Or what you say I can't do,

'Cuz God has His hands in this

And I know He'll bring me through.

It may look like my life is falling apart,

And nothing is intact;

But that's when God will use me most

And that's a matter of fact.

I don't have to be perfect,

Nor do I have to be right;

For God's love is brighter

Than any darkness in the night.

So whether you hate on me or believe

That this is as good as it gets,

I'm here to tell you

That God ain't through with me yet!

# Don't Quit

When times get hard,

And I know they will,

Don't throw in the towel

Just wait and be still.


When it seems like

The pain won't go away,

Read God's Word,

Repent and pray.


When it seems like

Your storm will never end,

Turn to God

He's your Comforter and your Friend.


When it seems like

Life is not worth living,

Hold on because

Jesus is the reason for your being.

You will make it through

You gotta believe it;

Whatever you do my friend,

Just don't quit!

# To All My Single Ladies

It ain't easy being single;

It ain't easy being alone.

It ain't easy having to live this life

All on our own.


But what are we willing to sacrifice

A job, our dreams, for a diamond ring?

Because if it ain't from God,

Then it ain't worth a thing.


I know it ain't easy,

Nor is it fun

To have to go year after year

Without someone.


But is it really worth

A kiss or even sex

And still have nothing in your heart

As you look for the next?

'Gon ahead and give it up

To that man who ain't worth jack

Only to satisfy an emotional lust

And then wish you had it all back.


Forgive me my sistahs

If this sounds too simple

But according to 1 Corinthians 6:19

Our body is a temple.


We are precious to God

In case you didn't know

He has our best interests at heart

And loves us so.


Ladies, God wants so much more

Than for us to settle for less

Because the man that He has for us

Will be nothing but the best!

Please listen to me ladies

As I spit this rhyme

Don't give any more of these godless men

A second of your time.

What do you have to lose you say?

Everything—your whole life is at stake;

Trust in the Lord with all your might

And in the end, it'll be worth the wait!

# Worthy to be Loved

I've waited all my life

To be loved by a man,

Someone who loves me for me

And is my very best friend.

A man who tries to understand me,

Who gets me and wants to be with me.

A man who will respect me and wants the best for me.

A man who will fight for me even in the roughest times.

A man who will encourage me and put me first.

A man who will protect my heart at all costs.


I thought I have found such a man.

One that was sent from God and was

Created just for me.

We spent time together,

We talked,

We laughed,

We cuddled.

But then in a blinking of an eye,

He disappeared.

Was this the love that I have always desired?

Was this the love that God wanted me to have?

I do not know what I did to deserve such pain.

I am lost in love,

And it hurts so badly.

I do not deserve to be treated this way.

I do not deserve to be kicked to the curb

As if I am meant for dogs.

Or treated like waste

I do not deserve

To have my heart broken in two,

To be stomped on, misused, and abused

Or to be treated as if

I am not worthy to be loved.

God loves me

This I know to be true.

I just want a real man

Who would love me too.

Who loves me and cares for me

As I will do the same,

Who fights for me and protects me

As he calls me by name.

The love we share

Would be evident to others,

And that no man or woman

Could ever come asunder.

I thought I found such a man

Who was faithful and true.

But instead of loving me,

He has left me sad and blue.

Oh how I wish I was worthy of love

A match made in Heaven

And sent from above.

He is out there somewhere

Please don't come in disguise

He will rescue me

And catch me by surprise.

If he loves God first

Then he can love me

We'll grow together, pray together

And raise a family.

I am worthy to be loved!

# Breaking Down the Walls

Why is it so hard for you to let people in?

You have so much potential lying dormant within,

Yet you hide yourself and keep others from coming in.

I know that you've been lied on, talked about,

Mistreated and abused

It makes sense that you are tired of being used.

But these weights are far too great to carry

It does you no good to have all this pressure

The wall that surrounds you is stronger than brick

I want to help you but I don't know how.

Piece by piece, I try to chisel my way through

Only hoping to get closer to you

But you push me to the side with every roll of the eye

If only I could show you that I'm not like all the others;

I implore you to let me show you that I'm different than they

I want to encourage you, pray with you, and show you some love

But the words I say are not enough

Over the years you have learned to shut people out

Your chances have been all used up

If only you had just one more left

I would show you the love that only Christ can give

Real, agape love that no man can fulfill

Real love that can withstand even the toughest wall

Just one more chance is all I need

To show you that this is no way to live

To shut out the people who care about you

Will only keep you further from Him;

With every tear you shed

He understands

He's here to hold you in His arms

And grant you with peace

He sees your hurt;

He feels your pain

He knows all you've been through

He wants to wrap you in His arms and never let you go

He wants you to be free from all the bondage you are in;

Be free to laugh, love, live, and give

Of yourself, I know there is more of you than you have shown me

I was sent here to tell you there is purpose in your pain

Allow God to comfort you and assuage your pain

In time, He will reveal Himself to you

And, with patience I believe that you will enjoy the real you

Not the one hiding behind the wall,

But the one who Christ wants to rebuild.

He wants to clean you up and make you brand new.

In Him, you are a new creature

The old has gone, the past is forgotten

Little by little, you too will see

That you will no longer be haunted by your past

God wants to heal you of your scars

He will give you a new body,

One laced with supernatural power.

For anyone who wants to get to you

Must go through Him first

Because God plus one is the majority.

Though, He alone is all you need.

He will fight the battles you don't have strength to fight.

You are more than a conqueror

Scarred and wounded,

But never defeated;

He's got you, He has covered you

By His stripes, you are made whole.

Just one more chance is all you need

To be freed from all your misery.

I want this for you

But you need to want it too.

I can't wait to walk with you in victory

For allowing God to work in and through you

The near is so close I can taste it;

I'm going to sit back and watch God at His best

Pebble by pebble,

Stone by stone,

Brick by brick,

He is chiseling His way through

I can see your walls are breaking down

I'm so relieved you've allowed a toe in and

You've granted me a chance to share this with you.

A new body, a new heart, a new life

Will be yours and soon you will see

That life is better than what you were dealt

Because in Jesus, you can't lose.

# I Can See Clearly Now

*I don't know who I am*

*Or where I'm going;*

*I don't know how much longer*

*I can go on.*

*No matter how hard I try,*

*I can't do anything right;*

*Every step I take*

*Leads me to a dead end.*

*Sometimes I feel like*

*I'm walking in circles;*

*Other times I feel like*

*I'm walking backwards.*

*I can't breathe;*

*I can't see.*

*The world is spinning*

*But I'm standing still.*

*I can't keep up*

*In this fast-paced society.*

*Everyone is moving swiftly*

*While I'm moving in slow motion.*

*What is happening to me?*

*I can't eat,*

*I can't sleep.*

*I don't know who I am*

*Or where I'm going,*

*Somebody please help me!*


I CAN HEAR YOUR CRIES

FROM DOWN BELOW;

I LOVE YOU MORE

THAN YOU'LL EVER KNOW.

I CREATED YOU AND

DEPOSITED YOU IN YOUR MOTHER'S WOMB.

FOR YOUR LIFE,

I HAVE A PURPOSE;

DON'T GIVE UP NOW

OR YOU'LL NEVER KNOW IT.

KEEP ON TRYING

AND KEEP ON BELIEVING,

FOR I AM HERE

AND WILL PROTECT YOU FROM HARM.

THOUGH TIMES WILL GET ROUGH,

I HAVE THE INGREDIENTS TO MAKE YOU STRONG,

STRONG IN HEART,

MIND, BODY AND SOUL.

SO OPEN YOUR EYES AND

I WILL RESTORE YOUR SIGHT.

THERE IS LIGHT AHEAD

WITH MANY OPEN DOORS;

TRUST ME, MY CHILD

FOR I AM WITH YOU ALWAYS

AND I LOVE YOU SO!


Thank You, Lord

For allowing me to see

The many blessings

You have given me.

I have a mind to think,

A heart to believe,

Feet to walk,

Legs to praise,

Arms to raise,

Hands to clap;

Lord, You have

Given me so much.

Thank You for

Opening up my eyes

So I can see reality.

I love You

And I trust You.

I will not quit

No matter how hard it gets.

I thank You for

Creating me and for

Loving me just the way I am.

I can finally see

The real deity.

Thank You, Lord

For I can see clearly now!

# Virtuous Woman

A wife of noble character

Who can find?

She is worth far more than rubies

She is truly divine.

She has confidence in her eyes

And poise in her step;

She utters no lies

All promises kept.

Her smile is so bright

It could light up a room;

Any man would be proud

Just to be her groom.

She works very hard

And is a devoted wife,

A nurturing mother

Who cares about life.

She's a woman

Virtuously,

A virtuous woman is she.

She speaks with wisdom

And faithful instruction is on her tongue;

A good woman is hard to find,

She comes second to none;

She lives life to its fullest

Taking nothing for granted,

Building relationships with others,

Even the disenchanted.

What an awesome delight

To be in her presence;

The way she moves and speaks

Is mere elegance;

From her style of dress

To the nails on her hands,

From the way she combs her hair

To the way her feet moves when she dances.

She's a woman

Virtuously,

A virtuous woman is she.

She sets about her work vigorously,

Her arms are strong for her tasks;

She sees that her trading is profitable

And her lamp always lasts.

She is always humble

And always meek;

When times get tough,

It is God she seeks.

She never gives up

Nor is she ever defeated;

All this beauty within her,

Yet never conceited.

Knowing the woman

God has called her to be,

She stands tall and proud

One of integrity.

She is a woman

Virtuously,

A virtuous woman is she.

She's a woman

Virtuously,

A virtuous woman

Is who I strive to be!

## Author's Notes

# SALVATION

## You Don't Know

"You Don't Know" is inspired by God: Ecclesiastes 8:7-8, 10:12; James 1:19-20; I Peter 3:9. My goal was to witness to people who think they have time to get their lives right before God. The reality is we don't. We must do it NOW before it's too late!

## Look To Jesus

There is so much we, as people, can get caught up in by living in the world. Material things may seem nice for awhile, but eternally will not bring happiness. Real happiness is in Jesus! Refer to Matthew 6:19-20, 24.

## You Don't Know (Part 2)

This poem is a continuation of the 1st "You Don't Know." I wanted it to have the same message but with a different rhyme scheme.

## Who Are You?

I started writing "Who Are You?" as a witness of a saved person living in the world. These things I either experienced on the job, watched on the news, or heard from others. Once I got started, more and more things came across my mind. Finally I realized that everything we do in the world that is contrary to the Word of God, is because of and related to our sins.

## Trust Me

"Trust Me" is dedicated to anyone who is lost and without God. God is speaking to everyone and He is pleading that you come to Him with your problems. He wants to love you and for you to love Him unconditionally.

## The Good News

This poem represents the true gospel of Jesus Christ—news that is certainly worth hearing and is definitely good! "The Good News" is the story of Good Friday and Easter all in one.

## Count It All Joy

It's so easy to get bombarded and overwhelmed by life's setbacks. Life isn't easy, nor is it fair. But whatever happens in our lives, it's only a test and it's only for a moment. When we're faced with difficult times, we must thank God in the midst of our trials and look forward to the breakthrough. God is on our side no matter what. It's through our brokenness that we tend to fully surrender to Him, and in that, He can use us greatly! In all things, remember to "count it all joy!" Refer to James 1:2-6.

## Armor of God

"Armor of God" is taken from Ephesians 6. God has given us spiritual warfare to fight the many battles of Satan. There are many wrong ways to fight but God shows us in His Word the right way to fight. He gives us the proper tools we need to defeat Satan. With these 7 weapons of warfare, our armor is complete! Satan doesn't stand a chance.

## His Loving Grace

"His Loving Grace" was written during my freshman year at the University of Michigan in 1996. I had been saved for only a short period of time and I thought about all I had learned about God and how I felt about Him. The rest was a piece of cake!

## THE CALL

Today is the day to give your life to Christ. He's calling you, He's knocking on the door of your heart. My prayer is that you will let Him in! God bless you!

Make A Joyful Noise


# HONOR

## 'Til We Meet Again

This poem is dedicated to the loving memory of Katherine Marie Boykins BKA "Scooter," who was murdered in 1997. She and I went to church together and we talked a lot. I was in my 1st year of college when this happened and I didn't get a chance to go to her funeral. She was only 17 when she died (September 17, 1979-April 16, 1997). I will remember her always.☺

## Tribute To Daymon

This poem is dedicated to Daymon Mumford who was killed on December 9, 2007 at age 30. He was an innocent bystander waiting on his boss so that he could go home to his family. Instead, he was called home to be with the Lord as he was shot by a stray bullet. Daymon was just an all-around good guy who was loved by many. He will certainly be missed!

# 26 Angels

On Friday, December 12, 2012, the world was in an uproar after the malicious, senseless, evil tragedy that killed 28 people, including the young gunman in Newport, CT. Sandy Hook Elementary will go down in history as the 2nd most deadliest massacres in America. 1 man, with no particular motive, decided to kill his mother at their home, then 26 innocent victims at Sandy Hook Elementary School. 20 of the 26 victims were children, ages 6 & 7. He then turned the gun on himself.

It makes no sense why these people had to die; they will always be remembered and treasured in our hearts. My poem, "26 Angels," is my heartfelt message to that devastated community. I pray for them often and hope that families will find peace in the midst of the storm. This city will be the safest town in America, not because of extra security in the schools, but because there are now 26 angels looking after them!

# FEELINGS

## Alone

I wrote "Alone" while I was in high school. It was a time in my life when I was depressed. I felt that nothing was going right and even though I was healthy, I was not happy. There were people in my life who tried to make me happy but I wasn't feeling them. This period of my life was before Christ and praise God it was transient.

I hope this poem speaks to those who feel or may have felt this way at some point in their lives. YOU ARE NOT ALONE! The good news is it won't last forever.

## Take Me Away

"Take Me Away" was inspired by a painting by Jameil Rasheed (1990) of a little girl living in a violent, poverty-stricken society. The poem is her cries to God.

## Crumbling

"Crumbling" is about the feeling we get when we are in deep, emotional pain and we feel as if we cannot go on. The pain continues to eat away at us, muffles our mouths, and numbs our bodies. We feel hopeless and we have nowhere to turn. This poem is a cry for help to the Lord to mend the broken heart and to be restored.

## Feelings

"Feelings" is about the unknown. Communication is key for any relationship to work. If one or both people aren't willing to express themselves then it opens up the mind for imagination, leading to confusion and hurt. You both owe it to each other to be true.

# RELATIONSHIPS

## What Is This Thing?

This poem is an expression of my feelings about a man of whom I thought was "the one." We hit it off in the very beginning but then it went awry. Once we met for the first time and then nothing was right thereafter. The more I got to know him, the more I realized he wasn't for me. I don't regret talking to this person because he is a part of my story, and he is a good person just not good for me.

## Free

"Free" is an expression of my true feelings to God regarding a relationship I once was in. I experienced conflicting emotions as I processed whether or not I should be with the person. My heart wanted it but my mind was not so sure.

## Shame On Me

I wrote this poem after breaking up with who I thought was the "love of my life." I had to first acknowledge that the feeling was not mutual. I had poured my heart out to this person until I had nothing left. He did not want my love and he no longer deserved anything I had to give. It was a horrible experience-loving someone who doesn't love back-but I am a better and stronger person today because of it .

# SELF-WORTH

## I Am What I Am

This poem is a reminder to myself that I am special to God. He created me as I am and He loves me for me. I should never compare myself to others because we are all equally special to Him. Flaws and all, we should love the skin we're in and know that God does not make mistakes!

## In His Eyes

"In His Eyes" defines our self-worth. We are unique, we are special, we are loved. Knowing these facts, we should want to do well and live for Him. There is nothing we could do to make Him love us less, so we might as well try our hardest to be the best we can be for Him. Others may see us one way, but the way God sees us is most important.

## The Beautiful Me

"The Beautiful Me" is for every person who dislikes the skin they are in. That used to be me. I try to focus less on my flaws (we all have them) and focus more on the good God created in me. I am beautiful and so are you!

## God Ain't Through With Me Yet!

This poem is for anyone who is judgmental or overly critical of others. No one is perfect; we all are works in progress. For everyone else, I hope that you will see the value in yourself and appreciate your worth because you are special to Him.

## Don't Quit

"Don't Quit" is dedicated to all those who feel like giving up. Life isn't easy. We have so many disappointments and failures, but the show does not stop there. In order to press forward, we must not look back, rather learn from our mistakes and look forward to our future. God spoke to me in this poem because many times I want to quit. But He lets me know that He loves me (and you too), and He will never leave me. All I have to do is believe and trust Him. They say that "the grass is greener on the other side" and "this too shall pass!" Refer to Philippians 3:12-14.

## To All My Single Ladies

This poem is dedicated to all the single ladies. Don't sell yourselves short. Don't give more of yourselves than you ought because a lot of men out here don't deserve any part of you. God created you for a purpose and with a purpose; you are valuable to Him. Be patient and wait on the one He has for you!

## Worthy to be Loved

Unfortunately this poem was written after a bad break-up, one in which I thought that I had finally found "the one," and watched as he walked out of my life. He took my heart with him and I felt unlovable for awhile. But then I realized that God loves me unconditionally and will hand-pick the man for me. He will give me what I need and want. I have to be patient because I AM worthy to be loved!

## Breaking Down the Walls

I once had a close friend who went through a rough time in her life. As much as I tried to talk to her, the more she pushed me to the side. I felt hopeless because she did not want to let me in. She had these invisible walls up that separated her from the rest of the world. At the end of the day, God is always available when you feel no one else is. He will restore you and give you beauty for your ashes. He will take away your pain and make you brand new. Life will have its share of troubles but you are not by yourself. Reach out to Him and to others.

## I Can See Clearly Now

"I Can See Clearly Now" is written for anyone who feels that life is not worth living, or, for those who don't know what their purpose is in life. God is powerful. He loves us even in the midst of our worst days. He created us for a purpose. It's up to us to trust Him and believe that He will reveal it to us. Praise God!

## Virtuous Woman

"Virtuous Woman" was taken from Proverbs 31. I enjoy reading Maya Angelou's "Phenomenal Woman," and I thought it would be a great idea to put together something similar to that of a virtuous woman—the way God wants us to be.

# ABOUT THE AUTHOR

Mendi Joi Wilson has enjoyed writing since she was a young girl. Her love for poetry flourished during early adolescence. Mendi loves God, self, family, friends, and people.

Mendi is a licensed professional counselor for the state of Ohio (LPC) and has provided counseling for numerous children and their families since 2010. However, she has worked with children in various settings most of her life. Mendi knew since she was a child that she wanted to teach, mentor, nurse or counsel children. Like most children whose future aspirations change, Mendi wanted to be a teacher, an author of children's books, a pediatrician, and now a counselor. Although the careers may have changed over the years, her passion for children has not.

Not only is her love for children great, but she loves people, in general. She cares a lot and is willing to help those in need. It pains her to see other people hurt and she strives to be the best person, woman, daughter, friend she can be. Though often quiet in nature, Mendi enjoys being around people, especially those who have things in common with her. She particularly loves going to church, singing in the choir, line dancing with friends, and even karaoke. Mendi enjoys playing sports and board games. She is willing to try anything once as long as it is not detrimental to her health and/or overall well-being,

Mendi is a believer and loves Jesus Christ as her personal Lord and Savior. She desires that all people will grow to love Him so that the world would be a much happier, safer, and peaceful place. Until then, Mendi will continue loving people as Jesus does, extending grace, patience, and forgiveness. Although she is far from perfect, she strives to be better every day and encourages others to do the same.

"Make A Joyful Noise." is Mendi's first publication. The poems are from her heart and stretch as far as high school years. It is a compilation of her work that she wants people to see what she has been holding onto all these years. The poems are geared toward the young reader or the young at heart. Mendi hopes that everyone who picks up the pages will experience God's love penetrating through the pages of the book and will be encouraged.